Contents

Note:

The omission of a glossary is deliberate. There are many readily available glossaries of computing terminology, and the casual reader can refer to these. As emphasised in the text, the serious reader should be careful to obtain expert advice on matters outside his own specialisation.

Hardware

1 Technical considerations

Introduction 1.1

Technical considerations refer to the computer installation itself — the environment in which it operates, its hardware, software, support services — from a contractual viewpoint and for a successful installation. Failure through lack of information has caused installations to come to grief because occurrences had been overlooked in the contractual arrangements. As computers become more the nerve centre of an organisation, even minor failures can have far reaching effects but a major failure can stop business operations completely unless the installation contracts are well planned from the beginning.

This publication does not set out to be a text book on this subject but attempts to draw attention to problem areas and thus provide guidelines and a checklist necessary to make the most effective use of computer facilities and to safeguard the installation.

Contractual installation implications arise long before actual installation and may even be a matter for consideration during the initial computer feasibility stage. Every aspect of the installation, whether hardware, software or support services has some pre-installation implications.

The introduction of a computer not only introduces new situations, but it can also draw attention to inadequacies in existing situations.

The problem of planning/reviewing computer installations is that no organisation is static and it is important to ensure that installations and contractual requirements are kept under review on a continuous basis. It is also important for installation managers to notify their legal advisor of changes. Large organisations may employ an official responsible for legal matters who would be aware of the need for consultation and be competent to specify precise requirements. In smaller organisations the need for consultation is even greater.

Environment   1.2

Equipment

It is necessary to specify all equipment characteristics that relate to the creation of the installation environment. The weights of units, both packed and unpacked, should be specified as relevant to floor loading (*see structural below*). A knowledge of equipment dimensions is essential to planning of installation layout and access routes. Features such as cable length may impose constraints on equipment siting. The amount of heat dissipated from units, both individually and collectively, is relevant to climatic considerations (*see climatic below*).

Electrical

The electricity required for each unit, and for the installation as a whole, should be specified. Information should include frequency, number of phases and acceptable tolerances. An indication should be given of the maximum total of electrical power drawn from the mains in extreme, well-defined circumstances: this will enable the user to assess the adequacy of his supply. The number of required power points should be specified with information on siting and type. Lighting requirements should be defined, including the need for test lamp points and other provisions.

Climatic

Climatic requirements are determined in part by the heat dissipated by the individual units and by the installation *in toto*. It is necessary to specify acceptable tolerances on temperature and humidity, filtration and cooling provisions, and whether an office environment without air conditioning can accommodate the installation.

Structural

The loading capacity of the floor should be specified, and whether spreaders are needed: if so, their characteristics should be given. Any provision for equipment mobility (eg castors) should be specified. Requirements for a raised floor should be defined, with information on siting, the position and number of access points, support structures, flooring materials, etc. Information should also be included on door widths, lifts, hatches, and storage areas for consumable materials and maintenance tools/equipment.

Security and protection
Provisions to cope with possible hazards should be specified, eg the effects of fire, flooding, explosion or acts of malice should be defined. The characteristics of automatic fire detection and prevention equipment should be included. It is also necessary to specify the need for fireproof cabinets, warning systems and emergency cut-out facilities. Provisions to counter unauthorised personnel access should be defined.

Installation commissioning 1.3
It is necessary to specify in full the circumstances of the commissioning procedure. For example, on what date will the equipment be delivered? How long will it take to install? At what time will the supplier be able to transfer operating responsibility to the user? The types of commissioning trials to be undertaken must be determined. What form will the trials take and how long will they last? It is also necessary to specify in detail the criteria whereby the trial results can be evaluated. At what point is the commissioning procedure to be judged complete?

Hardware 1.4

Equipment characteristics
It is required to itemise every unit of equipment and to specify all the features not already covered by *1.3*. Information should be included on equipment compatibility with other hardware. Can the units be physically linked to other equipment? Can they use common software? Performance data should be included to help assessment of the suitability of the hardware for the anticipated workload. Any previous use of the equipment should be made clear, with details of ownership, history and other relevant information. Data relating to the trade-in value of the current system should be included.

System expansibility
Appropriate information should be provided on the scope for system expansibility. Information on the capacity of the central processor(s) should be given to help user evaluation of the ultimate power of the configuration:

this data will relate to core size, tape and disc speeds, number of possible peripherals, etc. An indication should be given of whether system changes can be made on site and how long they would take. The availability of extra facilities should be made clear as relevant to possible future expansion. Any restrictions on the use of peripherals on mainframes from other manufacturers should be specified: such restrictions may extend to software *1.5*.

Consumable materials

All necessary details on consumable materials — punched cards, printer ribbons, stationery, etc — should be provided. Restrictions on the use of consumables, whether arising from operational incompatibility or for other reasons, should be specified.

Maintenance

All maintenance provisions should be defined. What equipment will be maintained? What will be the frequency and nature of such maintenance? Day of the week or date in the month should be defined. Such details should be given for each item of equipment. The procedure for emergency and major repairs should be specified. There should be clear statement of the responsibilities of user and supplier for the provision of test equipment and tools, for the cost of spare parts, for the cost of maintenance labour, and all other charging matters. Responsibilities for maintaining a standard of serviceability, for notifying (*See 2.3*) and repairing defects and for remedying faults arising from equipment modification should be defined. The duration of the maintenance contract, with dates of commencement and termination, should be specified.

Software   1.5

System requirements

The software necessary for the operation of the user's equipment should be specified. It should be made clear whether the software is separately charged or included in the hardware price. Any required operating system should be described, with details on maximum store needed, whether the system is accessible to the operator, and the policy for issue of updates. The utility and housekeeping software required for day-today operation should be specified, and whether this software is available from the supplier. Information should be provided on software storage requirements.

Maintenance

It should be stated whether the software is maintained by the supplier and whether there is a charge. The user should also know whether maintenance is automatic or whether he has to apply for updates. Does the supplier undertake to provide regular information on software availability and maintenance? And what are the consequences, to user and supplier, of software failure to perform the necessary operations? It should also be made clear whether user modifications to supplier software affect the supplier liability.

Support services 1.6

Planning, advisory and training

The assistance to be made available by the supplier in planning and implementation of the user's system should be specified. All charging considerations should be made clear. For example, how much time is to be made available by the supplier's technical personnel to assist the user? The circumstances of any training arrangements should be well defined. Is training restricted to a particular field (eg programming)? Is accommodation and are facilities for lecturers included? How long is the training to last? Again, are the specialist provisions free? If not, how are the costs determined?

Program and file conversions

The user may require to convert existing programs for the new equipment. The feasibility of such conversion — together with details of available assistance, the source of such assistance, etc — should be specified. Detailed cost information should be made available.

Standby facilities

The supplier should nominate a convenient matching configuration for standby purposes and ensure that it will actually fulfil all requirements, eg hardware, software and time. There should also be a general undertaking to nominate further standby facilities, if required to do so in the event of equipment failure (see also 1.4).

Manuals and documentation

A list of required hardware and software manuals should be specified. An indication should be given of their scope. In all instances the additional costs, if any, should be defined.

2　Legal considerations

Introduction　　　　　　　　　　　　　　　　　　　　　　　**2.1**

The information contained in section 2 relates to the law in the United Kingdom of Great Britain and Northern Ireland, concluding with a brief reference to international contracts. Some relevant Acts of Parliament which relate to the area of contract are summarised in an appendix. Any detailed legal points should be discussed with a legal advisor. This section has been written for guidance only, so that the reader may gain some appreciation of the kind of legal detail to beconsidered in any contractual arrangement for the buying or leasing of computer hardware, related equipment, software and services.

The contract　　　　　　　　　　　　　　　　　　　　　　　**2.2**

If it is intended that the formal contract shall constitute the whole of the agreement between the user and the supplier, it is desirable that any written undertakings, representations, commitments or warranties made at any time prior to the contract being signed are reproduced in the contract.

If there is written into the contract a statement or warranty to the effect that all other undertakings are excluded, the legal effect of this should be ascertained.

Parties to the contract

The names of the parties should be correctly shown in full. It could be a fundamental term of the contract that the user is not a subsidiary or associate of any other body corporate with whom the supplier might not be willing to contract, and the user may be required to give a warranty to this effect if appropriate.

Government departments

If the user is a Government department, it should be made clear in the contract whether or not any other departments are also entitled to the benefit from the contract.

Date

The date on which the title to each separate piece of equipment is to pass to the user is important for the calculation of depreciation, insurance and tax allowance. The date when the title passes to the user may differ from the *VAT* 'tax point'.

Price

The total price to be paid for the equipment and a detailed breakdown of the items with their individual prices should be given. It should also be made clear whether the price includes such items as transport, installation, technical advice and support, training, maintenance and software; and, if not, how much these will cost.

Any provision in the contract for a variation in price in the event of an increase in cost to the supplier between order and delivery should be examined. Note: It is particularly important that contracts for hire or lease should be explicit on the matter of the supplier's right to vary charges.

Payment

The contract should specify the following:

> The date when payment is due
> In the case of instalment payments, the dates when each instalment is due
> The rights of the supplier on non-payment of all or part of the price and until payment of the final instalment.

Note: In international contracts, place and currency of payment should be stated (*See 2.12*).

Interest charges

The contract should state any provision for a charge of interest on any part of the price which is unpaid, the rate of interest, the method of calculation (ie flat rate or reducing rate) and the true annual percentage rate.

Contracts for hire or lease

The contract should state:

> The commencement date and minimum period of hire or lease and any right to renewal
>
> The charges to the user and any rights of the supplier to change them
>
> The regular payment date
>
> Any rights of the supplier on failure to pay an instalment (*See under 2.2*).

As the title to goods will not usually pass from the supplier, the user should not assume any eligibility for tax allowances.

Assignment of contract

A contract will often contain a clause limiting the rights of the user to assign, sub-let or transfer the benefit of the contract, either forbidding assignment or requiring prior permission of the supplier (which it may be provided cannot be unreasonably withheld).

Note: A merger or takeover might affect the identity of the user and could resemble an assignment.

Definition of terms

Terms such as 'costs', 'equipment', 'software', 'contract', 'training', 'maintenance' and others capable of subjective interpretation should be precisely defined.

Warranties   2.3

Defects

Any warranty of freedom from defects should state the following:

> The period of the warranty
>
> The list of items included in the warranty
>
> The liability of the supplier in the event of defects developing
>
> On the position as to compliance with patent and copyright law (See 2.9).

Repair

In cases of a liability on the supplier to repair, the contract should state:
> whether he has the option to replace equipment instead;
> the effect, if any, of any failure by the user to report a defect within a
> specified time of its becoming apparent (*See under 1.4*).

Expense

If the contract places a liability on the user to meet any of the costs of
repair or replacement, the full nature and extent of that liability (eg labour
costs, spare parts) should be stated (*See under 1.4*).

Misuse

If a warranty clause excludes claims arising from misuse of the equipment,
the user should check that the purpose for which the equipment is to be
used does not itself amount to misuse, and should ask for a list of obvious
misuses.

Fitness for purpose, performance

A supplier has certain statutory liabilities as to fitness for purpose and
performance. With these in mind, the user should ensure:
> that the use to which the equipment is to be put is fully specified;
> that according to its specification the equipment is capable of fulfilling
> its intended purpose.

Limitation of liability   2.4

Exclusions

Any exclusion of the supplier's liability in the contract must be clear.

Expendable items are often excluded from a warranty.

Non-approved items

The user should consider the possible effect on the performance of the system
of using non-approved expendable items such as magnetic tapes, discs or
stationery (*See under 1.4*) and any limitation of the supplier's liability arising
from the use of non-approved equipment, spares or expendable items.

Time limit on legal action

The contract may contain a clause which limits legal action if not commenced
within a specified period and the Limitation Acts also impose such limits.

Cancellation and termination   2.5

Cancellation before the contract has become fully effective
If a significant interval may elapse between the making of a contract and the effective performance of it, the contract may contain provisions for the adjustment of prices or hiring charges (*See under 2.2*). If these operate, consider whether the user should have the right to cancel. Such a contract may also contain an escape clause if delivery or supply conditions override the control of the supplier, making performance impossible or even merely onerous. Such conditions should be clearly specified. The financial consequences in relation to payments already made or expenses already incurred should be stated in detail.

Cancellation may be possible under the general law of contract in other circumstances, for example total failure of consideration or anticipatory breach but such factors lie outside the scope of a guide.

Termination during the currency of a contract of sale
Termination of a Contract of Sale after acceptance of the goods and the passing of title to them will normally be governed by the general law as to breach of contract but it is desirable that the consequences should be considered and possibly provided for in the contract (*See 2.6*).

Termination during the currency of a contract of hire or lease
The following details should be stated in the contract:
The right of either party to terminate within the period of hire or lease whether for breach of a term or warranty, the period of any notice exercising such a right, how the notice is to be given (eg ordinary post, recorded delivery, etc.) and to whom it is to be given, where and when.
A statement that the notice is to be deemed conclusively to have been delivered on the date when, in the normal course of post, it should have been delivered can be helpful in avoiding disputes on dates.

Rights and obligations
The following should be stated:
The rights of the supplier or lessee on the breach of any obligation, eg should the supplier be entitled to terminate the contract on failure to pay an instalment on the due date.
What rights and obligations, which have already arisen between the parties, or between one party and a third party, arising out of the

contract, should be preserved in the case of a breach

If a breach can be remedied, whether the supplier is compelled to give notice of requirement to effect a remedy within a stated period of time before being entitled to terminate.

Any rights and obligations to repossess the equipment in the event of termination should be noted in the contract.

Damages   2.6

Liability

The following matters should be made clear:

The respective liabilities of the user and the supplier for loss or damage caused to either party or to third parties by any breakdown or accident in relation to delivery, installation and acceptance procedures.

The possible effects of defective equipment and loss of use resulting in consequential loss.

Any monetary limit to be placed on compensation for consequential loss. Note: Compensation cannot usually be obtained for consequential loss which the offending party could not reasonably have foreseen.

Liquidated damages and penalties

There may be a clause in the contract which provides that, in the event of any breach, damages, either of a stated amount or to be calculated at a stated rate, shall be payable. This is effective only if it can be shown by the claimant that the clause reflects a genuine pre-estimate of the probable loss resulting from a breach. If this cannot be shown (eg because only one figure is mentioned although the loss suffered as a consequence of one breach would be serious, but of another quite trivial) the clause may be construed as a penalty clause, intended to coerce rather than compensate. It would then be unenforceable.

Compensation

If either the user or the supplier has any right to claim compensation on cancellation or termination for any reason this should be clearly stated in the contract (*See under 2.5*).

Expendable equipment

If the supplier stipulates that certain items of expendable or ancillary equipment must be of a certain manufacture, breach of such a stipulation may give rise to liability in damages. Note: This is a different situation from that

(*Stated under 2.4*) where the performance of the system is affected by the use of unsuitable materials.

Equipment 2.7

Acceptability
If the transfer of title is dependent upon acceptance tests, these should be adequately specified and perhaps a maximum period for their completion given in the contract (*See 1.3*).

Installation
It must be made clear who is responsible for ensuring the operational feasibility of the installation and any modifications this may involve (*See 1.3*).

Removal
Any conditions relating to the location of equipment and any restrictions on change of location should be noted; also whether prior notification of change is required, and whether removal and reinstallation may be carried out only by specified people.

Maintenance
The following should be stated:
> A clear definition of the nature, scope and duration of any liability for the maintenance on all items of equipment
> Details of any separate charge for any part of the maintenance.
> Details of any actions on the part of the user which may render the maintenance undertaking invalid (*See under 1.4*).

Care of equipment
Where appropriate the user's responsibility for the proper care and housing of the equipment may be made explicit in the contract.

Abatement of price
Any relationship between a maintenance agreement and a warranty of freedom from defects for a specific period should be clearly stated.

Insurable risks 2.8

Attention has been drawn elsewhere to the need for clarity as to which party is liable for various risks. That party should take a considered decision whether or not to insure in the cases listed below. Sometimes there may be no option —

insurance may be a contractual or statutory requirement:

> Damage to or loss of equipment and third party liabilities arising
> between the signing of the contract and completion of delivery and
> installation.
> Damage to property during delivery and installation
> Injury to employees during delivery and installation
> Loss or damage to hired or rented equipment due to fire and other
> insurable perils.

The insured must understand and carry out any obligations imposed by the
insurer which, if not carried out, may invalidate the insurance policy or at
least reduce the insurer's liability. The other party may wish the contract
to impose an obligation so to insure and to refrain from any act or omission
which might avoid the insurances.

Patent and copyright   2.9

Liability for infringement
Parties should consider the desirability of:

> Any warranty as to the right to allow use of the material (as not
> restrained by any patent or copyright) or
> an indemnity (full or limited) against any breach.

Defence of legal action
Consider whether either party is to be under any responsibility for defending
any suit brought against the user on grounds that equipment or software
infringes any patent or copyright.

Exclusion clauses
In the case of sales there may be a limitation of any warranty or representa-
tion as to title to the rights which the supplier has and his absence of knowledge of any adverse right (as contemplated by Section 12 (2) of the Sale
of Goods Act as amended by Section 1 of the Supply of Goods (Implied
Terms) Act 1973). However any express exclusion of the provisions of
Section 12 is void under Section 55 of the Sale of Goods Act as substituted
by the Supply of Goods (Implied Terms) Act, 1973.

Modifications
A licence to use the hardware or software covered by a patent or copyright
only authorises the use of the particular items covered by the Licence. The
same supplier or a third party may have a patent or copyright on another

item which closely resembles the one covered by the Licence. If the user
alters, by adding to or modifying, that which he is licensed to use, he may
create an exact replica of that which is protected by the other patent or
copyright. In such a case he will be in breach of that other patent or copyright and become liable accordingly. If it is a third party's rights which are
infringed, the user will then be liable. On the other hand, if it is another
patent or copyright of the supplier which is involved; then the user's position
could be protected by words in theLicence, authorising the user to make
modifications within set limits and on certain terms.

Notification
The user's responsibility (if any) to notify the supplier of any threat of legal
proceedings within a specified period should be stated, as also should any
responsibility to notify any infringement of which he is aware (whether or
not it may lead to legal action).

Disputes as to proceedings
Consider a provision for resolving whether proceedings should be commenced
or defended on an infringement. A clause may be inserted obliging a party
to concur in taking or defending such proceedings dependent upon a favourable
opinion of Queen's Counsel.

Costs
Liability for the payment of damages and costs incurred as a result of a claim
for infringement and not otherwise recovered, should be defined. The successful party in litigation is often out of pocket.

Rectification
Consider whether the supplier should undertake to remedy any proven patent
or copyright infringements by replacement or modification of equipment or
software. The contract may also cover the responsibility for the cost of
removal of the offending items.

Consequential loss
The user should also consider whether he will suffer consequential loss in the
event of the withdrawal of the equipment or the software as a result of
patent or copyright infringement. The contract should state the extent of
any liability by the supplier for such consequential loss.

Confidentiality of information   **2.10**

Definition
The contract should state explicitly in relation to each party what is to be held
as confidential by him (eg manuals, equipment, specifications, facts relating
to the user's business, prices).

Information which can be shown to be public knowledge will usually be
specifically excluded from confidentiality provisions.

Reasonable care
The contract should call for parties to exercise reasonable care in dealing with
confidential information. Any disclosure which occurs, despite such reasonable
care, may not be actionable but there may be an obligation to require third
parties to enter into similar undertakings as to confidentiality before making
otherwise authorised disclosure to them.
Note: Special problems may arise when national security vetting is necessary.

Disputes   **2.11**

Procedure
The contract should state the procedure in the event of any dispute. In
international contracts it should select the "proper law" and venue. If
arbitration is to be used a clause should be so worded as to amount to a
"submission to arbitration" binding the parties to arbitration. A submission
to arbitration should state how the arbitrator is to be selected and in what area
the hearing is to take place.

Costs
If there is a clause providing for apportionment of costs between parties in
the event of the settlement of a dispute by arbitration or litigation, the user
must consider whether this is acceptable or whether the English practice
of costs being awarded by the arbitrator or the Court is preferable.

International contracts   **2.12**

Payment
The contract should state the currency in which payment is to be made,
whether either party has the option to nominate currency of payment, and
the place and terms of payment.

European Economic Community (EEC)

In contracts (or even gentlemen's agreements) involving parties based in
member states of the EEC there must be no condition which has a tendency
to inhibit competition between such states unless the agreement can be
brought within the exemptions.

Exchange control

In all cases, Exchange Control legislation of the country of the paying party
may prevent or restrict payment and an agreed procedure in such cases should
be considered.

Appendices
Relevant legislation

1 Misrepresentation Act, 1967

Preliminary discussions may contain oral or even written representations by or on behalf of the supplier of the goods which might fairly be said to have induced a contract. Even if parties were never truly in agreement on the matter, the supplier may, under the Act, be liable in damages to purchaser for representing something which later proves incorrect. The Act limits the power of parties to exclude liability for such representations. Such exclusion is only effective if the court considers it fair and reasonable in the circumstances of the case. Care should be taken to set out, in detail, in the contract document, the offer and basis on which it is made. Stipulation may be included in contract that nothing which is not recorded in the contract should be deemed to constitute an inducement to the contract and therefore any other statements or representations are to be regarded as withdrawn. If grossly erroneous statements are made in preliminary negotiations, any attempt to avoid liability is likely to be ineffective.

2   Trade Descriptions Act, 1968

In relation to contracts for sale or supply of goods (for 'services' see below) it is an offence to apply false trade description to goods or to supply goods to which a false trade description is applied (for example: as to size, method of manufacture, fitness for purpose, results of testing, history of previous ownership). A trade description is false if it is false to a material degree. 'Goods' will include hardware and usually software. False description need not be a contractual term. Care should be taken in describing goods in pre-contractual negotiations, in contract, and also in any written particulars supplied with the goods. An infringement does not necessarily affect the contractual position of parties. It gives rise to criminal liability.

Similarly, it is a criminal offence for any person, in course of trade or business, either to make a statement which he knows to be false or recklessly to make a statement which is false, in relation to supply of services, etc., provided in the course of trade or business.

3 Supply of Goods (Implied Terms) Act, 1973

This Act does not apply to services or international contracts. It curtails the freedom to exclude liability for terms which are implied by statute in a contract for the sale of goods. Liability on such implied terms may not be excluded in consumer sales (broadly speaking these are "sales for private consumption"). In non-consumer sales, any such exclusion of liability except as to title, is enforceable only where it is fair and reasonable in all the circumstances, including those which caused acceptance of the exclusion.

4   Fair Trading Act, 1973

This Act extends the Restrictive Trade Practices Act, 1956, bringing in agreements relating to patent and design pooling. It can be extended, by Order, to restrictive or information agreements between suppliers of services.

5   Consumer Credit Act, 1974

Bear this Act in mind when making a credit agreement, unless "debtor" is a
body corporate or alternatively an unincorporated association consisting
entirely of bodies corporate. A *consumer credit agreement* is one whereby
credit or financial accommodation up to a maximum of £5,000 is supplied to
an individual partnership or unincorporated association. Unless an agreement
is an *exempt agreement* under S.16, it is a regulated *agreement. Exempt
agreements* include those where a number of instalments other than down-
payment does not exceed three or, in certain circumstances, where credit
charge is 10% or less, or where agreement has connection with a country
outside the United Kingdom.

Regulated agreements are governed by requirements and restrictions of the
Act, for example, rights of withdrawal and cancellation. Transactions linked
to a *regulated agreement,* for example maintenance contracts, are also affected. A person or body who carries on a business of granting credit under
regulated agreements must be licensed by Director of Fair Trading. A person
is not to be treated as carrying on a particular type of business merely
because occasionally he enters into transactions belonging to business of that
type. Cost of credit, which includes a pure interest element and all other
borrowing costs (including those incurred by a debtor under ancillary contracts
for services where the debtor is not free to choose his own supplier of
services), will have to be stated in terms of true annual percentage rate.

Agreement for the hire of goods (but not services) may be regulated by the Act, if it may continue for more than three months and does not require payments exceeding £5,000. For details, obtain advice on the Act if you think you may come within it.

Software

Introduction

This Section is intended to help those who are involved in acquiring or supplying software. In preparing these guidelines, the authors have concentrated on the needs of that group of readers who may feel most in need of sound advice — those who are acquiring software for the first time — but regular buyers and suppliers should find it useful to have an independent source of informed comment. As can be seen from the list of contributors, the Section blends the views of professional purchasing managers, computer users, bureaux, hardware manufacturers, consultants, software suppliers and lawyers.

Although it is expected that this Section will be of value to software suppliers, and to others such as solicitors and company lawyers responsible for drafting software contracts, it is addressed in the main to the user. A buyer of software (whether packaged or bespoke) will often be presented with a standard form of licence or contract on a take-it-or-leave-it basis. The buyer needs to be able to understand the contract to make sure that the rights being granted, the obligations being assumed, and the products and services being acquired, are what are expected, and represent reasonable value for the money being paid.

Standard form software contracts offered by a supplier are not necessarily immutable. Whether it is possible to persuade a supplier to change his standard conditions depends on a number of factors — supplier's policy, relative bargaining strengths, total volume of business and so on. If a standard form contract is unreasonable or inadequate, nothing is to be lost by asking for it to be changed.

The Section has been divided into three parts — technical, commercial and legal. There is inevitably some overlap between them, but this should be seen more as belt-and-braces than unnecessary duplication.

Lastly, a warning — neither computing nor the law stands still, though they each develop at their own pace. Some of the statements contained here may become out-of-date.

A software contract should be looked at from the viewpoint of three different disciplines — computing, commercial and legal. If the contract is important enough, it should be checked by appropriate professionals from all these areas.

1   Technical

1.1   SPECIFICATION

This defines what the software does or what it is required to do. The cost, performance and schedules should be based on this, and the specification frozen or a date for a frozen specification agreed. This should include reference to sales literature, manuals or correspondence. Make sure the product has an adequate technical specification. The specification should define in detail the format and type of input data it is designed to accept and process and the output end result of its operation. The output should define the exact layout of the data and what each column or line of information means. The specification should also define the input medium (cards, paper tape, etc) and the output medium (print and printer, VDU, etc). (See 1.11 and legal section.)

1.2   ENVIRONMENT

If you know that you are going to change your operating system, hardware, terminals, teleprocessing software, etc, or duplicate the software on other manufacturers' hardware, then try to specify the future changes at the time of the initial input. If you might want to change the hardware, the number of terminals, etc, then decide at the outset how much flexibility you require in the initial version of the software. If the software is needed for specific times then make sure that the contract gives clear priority to delivery on time.

1.2.1 Hardware

This defines on which types of computer the software will run, the degree of inherent flexibility and any restrictions for multiple usage. Inherent flexibility might include ability to run on:

— other manufacturers' computers;

— bigger computer;

— smaller computer;

— next generation;

— with more users;

— with more terminals;

— with different terminals;

— with mixed terminals.

1.2.2 Software

This defines the operating systems and communication protocols and other software with which it will work or is required to work, and the degree of inherent flexibility. Inherent flexibility might specify:

— other operating systems from the same supplier or from different suppliers;

— different teleprocessing for database software, etc, as well as the items mentioned under hardware flexibility.

1.2.3 Language

Defines languages used or to be used when writing software and the language it supports. No change of language will usually be possible with package software. However, in the case of bespoke software it may be possible to have a choice, depending on the hardware used. The language finally adopted can usually be safely based on advice from the software suppliers in discussion with the hardware supplier. The language finally agreed should form part of the contract.

1.3   SECURITY

This defines the level of security against unintentional and intentional unauthorised intervention and how breaches will be corrected. It defines the onus on the user to avoid action liable to breach security or enable others to do so. The NCC *Management Handbook of Computer Security* describes the sort of matters which are relevant: 'When designing a system, measures must be taken which will identify both human error and malfunctions in the system, and minimise their effects. Programmed controls may be required to check the acceptability of input data and files, the correct functioning of program instructions, hardware operation and data handling, together with security measures to detect any accidental or deliberate misuse of data or malpractice within the system. These controls and security measures must be specified in detail at this stage, together with the procedures necessary to ensure their effectiveness

'The security of the system must be given careful consideration throughout the design process, from the systems analysis stage — when it is essential to base the feasibility study on a sound analysis of the existing (or required) system and on the needs of the user — to the question of future needs, when measures must be taken to allow the accommodation of future needs at a later date without loss of security'.

1.4   RESOURCE USAGE

This defines the importance of memory size, and utilisation, peripheral utilisation, run times and likely future requirements as needs increase. (See Section 1.11 on *slippage and over-run* and legal section.)

1.5   ACCEPTABILITY

Specify the method of testing to ensure that the program does what is defined under 'Specification', 'Security', 'Performance', and 'Documentation', and the action in the event of unacceptability in each area. It will be necessary to define the trial period from date of delivery.

1.6   PERSONNEL

This specifies who approves the personnel involved and their availability (both pre- and post-acceptance). This could apply to both technical and managerial personnel (both user personnel-to-supplier and vice-versa), including those utilised outside the prime shift. Whether or not you wish to interview staff will depend upon the size of the contract. The NCC would generally recommend interviewing in cases of a large contract.

In the case of bespoke software, user personnel designing the system may need in-depth access to company papers, systems and records. Hence interviewing may be held to be essential.

1.7   DOCUMENTATION

This defines the level of documentation and when it should be available and whether documentation is part of the total acceptability. It should also define the method and frequency of updating documentation. Finally, the different types of documentation to be supplied should be specified, ie user manuals, technical, operating and training. (See *Documentation of Software Products,* J D Lomax, NCC Publications, 1977.)

1.8   SOURCE CODE

To amend software requires access to source code.

Commonly, bespoke software is written for an individual

buyer, who pays for all of the development. Such buyers should arrange that they have contractual ownership of the source code, unless they give or sell rights to the suppliers or a third party.

Proprietary software supply may or may not provide for buyer access to source code. If an application package is to be added to or amended at the outset ('tailoring') then it may be sensible to consider the whole as being bespoke so far as access to source code is concerned, but with limitations on commercial exploitation rights.

Some of the most important contracts are for the supply of systems software which the buyer will use as a base for his development of applications. NCC's product, Filetab, is an example of such software. The supplier, in most cases, provides a full maintenance service, and for as long as the supplier continues to be able and willing to do this, the buyer should have no need to work on the source code. The contract should define the buyer's rights in the event of the maintenance service being withdrawn (the extreme case arises in the event of the supplier ceasing to trade). One answer is alluded to in Chapter 3, where the legal aspects of 'third party safe custody' (ESCROW) are discussed.

It is up to each buyer to decide how likely it is that source code amendment will be needed, but it should be remembered that virtually every major software product in the past has needed regular modification to ensure continued compatibility with the other systems software (especially, operating systems).

Unless the buyer feels that there is no chance whatsoever that access to the source code will be needed, the source code should be reviewed:

—   physical form (written, printed, magnetic tape, etc);

—   quality and convenience (language, structure, dependence on subsidiary software products);

— compatibility with various versions of operating systems and with other equipment.

1.9   MAINTENANCE

Specify:

— who is responsible for correcting errors;

— who changes to meet changed hardware;

— who changes to meet changed software;

— who is responsible for changing to meet government legislation and guidelines;

— the times and fee requirements to meet changed user requirements;

— the minimum time the commitment on the supplier lasts for enhancement, maintenance and maintenance changes;

— the availability of extension;

— the agreed procedure in the event of default or suspected fault including response time;

— the supplier's policy of support for the product;

— the steps taken to protect the user in the event of the supplier defaulting (deposit of annotated source, an 'escrow' arrangement). Permission for in-house correction and availability of an annotated source for such correction (see 1.8).

It is recommended that consideration be given to having pre-negotiated emergency procedures written into the contract.

1.10 TRAINING

This defines the availability and charges for user training to whom and to what standard of acceptability. (If the acceptance test is performed by user staff then training will be automatically incorporated in the acceptance test.)

1.11 SLIPPAGE AND OVER-RUN

This defines action to be taken when slippage in schedules or inadequate performance is detected, any periods of grace, the effect on acceptability and the financial and legal consequences.

1.12 SUPPLY

This defines technically the form of the initial supply of software and documentation. In the case of software this will nominate whether it will be on magnetic tape, disk, paper tape, or punched cards, etc. If possible it should similarly define the media for all subsequent amendments.

Any limitations during the trial period should be specified.

2 Commercial

2.1 INTRODUCTION

As has been mentioned elsewhere a prospective customer would be well advised to take up references and make additional enquiries. However, a buyer of software should obviously limit the extent of the enquiries to the value of the contract being negotiated. If a customer only needs the services of a couple of programmers for a few weeks, then it would be sensible to limit the pre-contract activities. At the other extreme a customer negotiating for a year's contract, value £2m, should obviously give considerable time and money to the pre-contractual discussions.

Customers may be presented with a 'standard contract', but a prospective customer seriously interested in obtaining a product or service should be able to get variations to suit particular needs. But once again the time spent on trivial or minor variations will depend upon the value of the transaction. Variations may also affect the price and delivery.

2.2 METHODS OF PAYMENT

The contract should specify the method of payment.

There are three possible methods:

2.2.1 Lease

Usually a payment made for an agreed period. The maximum is usually five years. Another fee is paid after a specified period and it will also be necessary to define as far as possible at this point the conditions which may govern any future fee payments such as discount terms. Usually no termination is possible until the end of the lease period.

Where a leasing arrangement is contemplated, the supplier should be appraised — will he be in existence for the length of the lease? (It is also important to ensure that software is needed for the length of the lease.) Escalation clauses are not usual in a leasing contract and should be avoided.

A down-payment and regular monthly payments may be better than a single payment: more negotiating strength could be retained in the event of customer dissatisfaction. Maintenance usually requires a separate contract.

2.2.2 Rent

Usually but not always this involves a monthly payment with an agreed notice to terminate on either side. There may be a minimum term before termination is possible. A rent arrangement is versatile in that it is easier to respond to changes in requirements. Also supplier standards can be ensured through withholding rent.

Rental involves fairly heavy investment in selection and set up. Care should be taken to avoid being 'locked in'. Escalation clauses and provisions for maintenance are usually included. Notice of termination usually depends on frequency of use (eg payroll might be 3 months, accounting suite 12 to 18 months).

2.2.3 Purchase

This usually means a single payment and is commonly used for small items of software and for some manufacturers' standard software. It is important to ensure what guarantees are included, eg on maintenance for a specified period. The liability for installation costs should be defined. With a large item, installation costs should be included.

2.3   DEVELOPMENT PAYMENTS

2.3.1 Time and Costs

This particularly applies to bespoke software. It usually means that the contract is open-ended as to price in that the supplier will bill the man-time expended and other specific costs incurred (eg computer time) on a monthly basis or at other agreed intervals. The maximum cost may be stated in the contract with an estimate of time to complete.

An 'open cheque' approach is not recommended, unless accompanied by strict controls. There must be agreed rates, and escalation clauses must be limited or controlled by reference to agreed indexes.

2.3.2 Fixed Prices

Where a fixed price contract is offered this may be the best method but this will usually be for 'normal work' which should be defined. However a customer should explore whether he could save money on 'normal work' by demanding charge rates and time estimates (and following up by requiring evidence of time expenditure).

The charging rate for 'extras and changes' may be much higher than the 'normal' rate. For instance, a customer may have certain obligations, such as to supply computer time or test data, and in a fixed price contract any delay on the customer's part may generate additional charges. It should be remembered that fixed prices may put too much of the planning power with the supplier.

2.4   MAINTENANCE

The cost and payment method should be specified. A regular monthly payment should be defined. This is especially important when software is supplied across national boundaries, eg is payment to be in the user's normal currency or that of the supplier (with attendant exchange fluctuation problems)?

2.5   NON-PAYMENT

The contract should state clearly the effect of non-payment or late payment either in the case of a licence fee or a progress payment for bespoke software. Does this involve any loss of rights or loss of use, and if so, for how long?

2.6   COMMERCIAL EXPLOITATION

2.6.1   Bespoke Systems

Users should consider whether the system being developed for them and to their specification is likely to be commercially exploitable. For this to be so, certain criteria will be preset:

— a serious marketing and sales effort supported by first rate brochures and other documentation

and either

— a technical lead (over the nearest equivalent software available from the computer manufacturer, for example)

or

— an applications lead; a fully developed and flexible range of functional capabilities (probably appropriate to a specific market segment; for instance, time accounting for solicitors).

If the system does appear to be commercially exploitable either by the buyer or by the supplier, the buyer should ensure that his rights are explicit in the contract.

The buyer may have no wish to market the system, but it may be to his advantage to restrict the supplier's right to use the software, or the concepts embodied in it, for other clients. In particular, it is reasonable for the user to expect agreement on a time-limited restriction so far as work for his competitors is concerned.

A supplier may wish to contract to supply the system prepared for one customer to others and offer the original purchaser a royalty on sales. This can be an acceptable method of recouping some development costs.

2.6.2 Proprietary Systems

In the case of proprietary systems — packages — the supplier is very unlikely to accept restrictions on his right to supply the client's competitors.It is still important, though, to have a non-disclosure clause covering the commercially secret aspects of the user's application of the package.

It is common for the supplier to seek restriction on the user's rights of use. For instance, restrictions may be to:

— one named installation;

— a named range of subsidiary companies;

— a specific territory or territories.

Should the user wish to extend his application of the package, he should be careful to obtain the supplier's prior agreement, otherwise he may find that the agreement and the licence relating to technical support are void.

3 Legal

3.1 INTRODUCTION

A software contract — indeed, any contract — is a setting down in writing of an agreement between two or more parties. It is important that the contract is clear not only to the people involved when the contract is signed, but also to those who may be involved subsequently. If you are not clear as to the meaning or interpretation of a particular contract clause appearing in a standard form of contract, then you should ask for an explanation, in writing. Any variation of the contract which is agreed during discussions should also be set down in writing. If all goes well, a contract can be put away as soon as it is signed and forgotten. It should be necessary to refer to it only when things start to go wrong. Even then, it is far better for misunderstandings and disagreements to be resolved by discussion than by quoting from a contract. Make sure, therefore, as far as you can, that the person or organisation with whom you are proposing to contract is reputable, sound financially and trustworthy.

If the user fails for any reason to sign the licence or contract, his use of the program will normally be taken to imply his agreement to the contract conditions. But if the supplier fails to sign, his agreement to the contract cannot be implied from the mere fact that the user has a copy of the program and is using it.

Much of the comment in this section is based on the following assumptions, neither of which, so far as we are aware, has been decided in a court of law, at least in the

United Kingdom. Despite this, they are believed to be well-founded, and were accepted in principle by, for example, the Whitford Committee in its report on Copyright and Design Law, published in 1977.

The assumptions are:

1   a computer program is a literary work within the meaning of the Copyright Act 1956;

2   the use of a computer program in a computer involves one or more of the following acts which are restricted by copyright:

—   reproducing the work in a material form;

—   making an adaptation of the work;

—   reproducing an adaptation of the work;

3   'adaptation' applied to a computer program includes conversion from any programming language into any other programming or intermediate language, or into machine-readable code or signals.

  Program documentation (which, together with the program itself, constitutes the software) is copyright work.

It follows from the assumptions that:

—   the 'author' of a computer program is normally entitled to the copyright in it, and therefore to the exclusive right to commit, and to permit others to commit, the restricted acts;

—   if the program is written by an author or authors in the course of employment under a contract of service, the employer is normally entitled to the copyright.

This latter point is important in contracts for developing

bespoke software. In the absence of other agreement, copyright in a program commissioned from and written by, for example, a software house, belongs to the software house, and not to the person or organisation who commissions the work.

Much of what follows will be better understood if the foregoing basic principles of copyright protection are borne in mind.

This section is divided into three parts. The first deals with the grant of rights — the licence to use; the second with the contractual conditions which normally accompany such a grant; and the third part deals with matters peculiar to a development contract.

3.2   GRANT OF RIGHTS

3.2.1 Use

The first essential in a software contract is a grant of a right to use the program, usually called a licence. It may be possible to imply a right of use even though it is not specifically spelled out in the contract; but do not rely on this. An explicit grant, apart from anything else, carries with it an implied warranty that the grantor has the right to make it.

A licence to use the program would imply the right to load and run it on a computer, but would not necessarily imply (for example) a right to make library copies. There should also, therefore, be a right to make copies. Usually the number of copies which may be in existence at any one time is limited, either to a specific number (eg five) or to the number necessary for use and operational security.

Non-Exclusiveness

A licence to use a software package will normally be non-exclusive. This may not be important unless you are acquiring the use of the package in order to offer an exclusive bureau service in a specific area, for example, or to steal a march on competitors. If you want exclusive rights of use, you will have to pay for them.

Non-Transferability

A licence may also be non-transferable, and this can create problems in the event of a merger or take-over. Generally it is better if the embargo on transfer applies 'except with the consent of the Licensor'. The Licensor, or software supplier, may not then withhold consent except on reasonable grounds.

Non-exclusiveness and non-transferability in relation to bespoke software are dealt with in 3.4.

3.2.2 Limitations on Use

Purpose

A licence will almost certainly place restrictions on the use of a program. There is, of course, a restriction on the purpose for which a program may be used which is inherent in the design of the program — a program cannot be used for any purpose for which it is unsuited. The contract may place other limits on the purpose of use — for example, only on the work of the licensee; for bureau work only on payment of additional fees; or for the work of the Licensee and its associated companies. Check that restrictions on use are not so onerous as to prevent you using the program for any present or likely future purpose.

Time

Another restriction on the right of use may relate to time. Some licences endure for the legal term of copyright (generally at least fifty years); others may be for stated periods, or be subject to termination by notice after a specified minimum period. Most contracts will have a clause providing for termination in the event of breach of contract by the Licensee; breach may include non-payment of fees or charges.

Make sure that you will have a right to use the program, provided you abide by the contract terms, for as long as you want it. If the licence is for a fixed term, you want a right to renew, with some safeguard as to the terms on which renewal will be agreed.

Computer

A third restriction on use is likely to apply to the computer on which the program is run. There is an obvious technical limitation here, in that a program may not run on an installation different from the one for which it was written. But a licence may impose even stricter limits, for example to a specified computer located at a particular address. If there is a possibility of a change in computer, or location, find out what, if any, costs or difficulties there may be in having the licence changed to cover the new machine or the new location. You may not get these included in the licence, but you may get a binding commitment to act in a certain way under specified circumstances. However, if the licence does limit the use of the program to an individually specified machine, it should also provide for use (without additional charge) on another machine in the event of a breakdown or non-availability during maintenance, repair, etc.

User

Usually, only the person or organisation named in the licence or contract is entitled to use the program. Specific permission for use by another (for example, a bureau providing a computing service during a changeover period) must be obtained, either in the contract or by separate letter or licence.

3.3   CONTRACT CONDITIONS

In addition to the grant of a right of use, a software contract should set out any other rights granted or available to the Licensee, and the obligations of both parties in relation to each other and possibly to third parties. It will also include various legal matters such as disclaimers, warranties, proper law, and arbitration.

3.3.1 Additional Rights

Modification

Probably, the most important additional right that a user of software might require is the right to modify it. This is particularly important for bespoke software, but may also be required for a packaged program.

Usually, whatever limits or restrictions apply to the unmodified program are also applied to any modification, and it is often a condition of the contract either that copyright in the modification will rest in the Licensor, or that the Licensor will have full marketing rights, with or without payment to the user who carries out the modification. If the modification consists of an identifiable set of program instructions which are additional to the main program, copyright in the modification may remain with the author — the Licensee.

Modifications to bespoke software are likely to be of value only to the user, and the important point to ensure in a contract is that there is a right of use. Modifications to a program package, however, may have considerable commercial value, and before embarking on a major modification the rights of both parties to the contract should be clearly ascertained or agreed — particularly the right of exploitation, and the right to a share of the income.

Although these remarks have been concerned largely with program modifications, they may equally well apply to documentation, since anything other than minor program changes will entail changes to manuals and listings.

Use by Third Parties

Bureaux using proprietary software may require the following rights which would not normally be granted to ordinary users:

— use of the software on work for third parties;

— use of the software by third parties (eg by remote terminal).

These additional rights may entail extra payments by the bureau, often by way of royalties.

Termination

Where the consideration for licensed rights consists of a series of periodic payments, make sure that you have the right to terminate the licence. You may have to give written notice to terminate (in which case payments will have to be made up to the end of the notice period), and on termination there may be a requirement to return to the Licensor all documentation and program copies, and to certify that the program has been deleted from the computer store.

3.3.2 Obligations of Licensee

Confidentiality

A software contract will almost certainly impose an obligation on the Licensee to keep the program, and perhaps some documentation, confidential. This will not prevent disclosure of information that has already been made public, but does make the Licensee liable for any loss or damage which the supplier of the software may suffer as a result of unauthorised disclosure of information about the software which may be considered secret or confidential. If there is a blanket embargo on disclosure, it will be up to the Licensee to show that information passed by him to a third party was public knowledge.

In most cases, a Licensee is a firm or corporation, and its own employees necessarily have access to confidential information. Such employees should have a provision in their employment contracts obliging them not to disclose confidential information. By the same token, the employer should make his employees aware of any programs or documents which are to be treated as confidential.

Despite all precautions, there is an ever-present risk that a determined dishonest or disgruntled employee (or merely a careless one) will pass on confidential information. The employer is liable for any loss or damage that may result, and it is unlikely that he will be able to obtain recompense from the employee. The possibility of insuring this risk should be examined.

Payment

Another major obligation of the Licensee is, of course, to pay any fees or charges. There may be only a single fee for a perpetual licence, in which case, once payment has been made, there is no further payment liability. But more frequently fees are payable monthly, quarterly, or annually; or the single fee may be for a limited term, at the end of which the licence expires unless renewed. The cost of a renewed licence may be lower (in real terms) than the cost of the original, and in some cases is a purely nominal sum. The licence will generally provide that failure to pay on a due date renders the licence liable to termination.

Miscellaneous

Other obligations often placed on the Licensee include:

— to report to the Licensor any suspected infringements of the copyright in the software (that is, any unauthorised use of the program, or copying of the program or documentation);

— to report to the Licensor any claim instituted by a third party for infringement of copyright;

— to assist the Licensor to protect his copyright and to defend any third party claim (this obligation should contain an undertaking that such assistance will be at the Licensor's expense);

— to allow the Licensor to verify that the software is being used only as permitted by the licence or contract, and that any royalties have been correctly paid;

— to provide an audited statement of royalties from time to time.

3.3.3 Obligations of Licensor

Supply

The first obligation of the Licensor is, of course, to supply the program and documentation. This might sound simple enough, but in fact it is the area where most problems can arise.

Performance

In the first place, the program should perform as it is intended to, and as the supplier says it will. It could be argued that, as the user of the program is not buying the program, but only the right to use it, the user has no protection under the Sale of Goods Act, as amended, or, indeed, any of the current consumer protection legislation. The user should try to ensure, therefore, adequate protection under the software contract or licence against inadequate performance of the program. The contract itself may not specify the program functions in detail, but these will appear in some at least of the accompanying documentation; generally, in the user manual.

Errors

Unless a program has been widely used over a fairly extended period it is unlikely to be free from errors, and there should therefore be an adequate error-correction service. The contract should state whether this service is free or, if not, how it is to be charged for.

Implementation and Training

Most programs need to be supported by implementation and training services. Details of these should be given in the contract, and again it should be made clear whether they are charged for or not.

Program Copy

The copy of the program needs to be in a format and on a medium that meets the user's requirements; this need not be specified in the contract (though it sometimes is) so long as the supplier is responsible for implementation.

Documentation

The contract should detail the documentation to be provided. Generally, with a packaged program, this will consist of a user manual, possibly with a separate operator's manual or operating instructions. If only one copy of the user manual is supplied, the right to make extra copies should be granted, or the terms on which further copies can be obtained from the Licensor should be stated.

Support and Maintenance

The obligations of the Licensor to provide services in connection with a program — error correction, implementation, training, and consultancy - may be contained in a separate contract from the program licence, and may be the subject of a separate charge or charges. A support and maintenance contract may not be obligatory on the Licensee, but often there is a strong financial incentive in its favour. There may be heavy charges for providing new program releases, advice on error correction, and consultancy to those not under contract.

3.3.4 Custody of Source Code

If annotated source code and associated documentation such as flow-charts are not supplied by the Licensor, the user should consider his position if the Licensor goes out of business for any reason. While the right of use will probably continue, error correction and updating services may no longer be available. Increasingly, the practice of a copy of the source code and documentation being held by an independent, disinterested party in safe custody for release to users in the event of failure of the Licensor to provide maintenance is being adopted. This practice has been called "escrow".

An escrow arrangement will usually involve the Licensor (supplier), and the Licensee (user), and the "escrow agent", and will be the subject of a separate agreement. This agreement should be examined in relation to the following:

— how to ensure that the deposited material is sufficient for the user to maintain his own software;

— how frequently the deposited material is up-dated;

— under what circumstances is the deposited material released;

— how soon can the material be released after failure of the supplier's maintenance service;

— what is the cost of the escrow service, and who pays;

— if the Licensor pays, what happens if he defaults.

3.3.5 Disclaimers

The supplier of a computer program — the Licensor — will naturally wish to avoid any unreasonable liability to the user. The user may have difficulty getting his money back, or making the supplier correct errors in the program, under present consumer protection legislation. The right to copy a program gives no more than the right to copy it as supplied, warts and all. However, a software contract normally goes further than this. Although the difficulties of enforcing error correction (in the absence of some contractual obligation) may remain, the user may have, in addition to any contractual protection, some right of redress for any loss or damage he may suffer as a result of a failure of the program to perform in accordance with its specification.

Although you may come across a contract condition, therefore, which states that the Licensor accepts no liability whatsoever for any damage or loss suffered by the Licensee as a result of using the program, or which sets a limit to the amount of liability, the condition is not necessarily enforceable. Both the law of negligence and the Unfair Contract Terms Act 1977 enter into this discussion, but it is not feasible in this booklet to consider in detail the validity of disclaimers of liability under present law. Perhaps it is sufficient to state that a disclaimer must be reasonable in the circumstances, and that the burden of showing that it is reasonable is placed on the supplier.

Despite the foregoing, a contract condition which seeks to limit the software supplier's liability should not be dismissed as of no consequence. If a claim should arise, the supplier will inevitably draw attention in the first place to the disclaimer, and the decision whether to seek redress through the law, or through arbitration, rests with the claimant. Either course can prove expensive and time-consuming, with no guarantee of eventual success: this is particularly so at present, when there are few, if any, guiding precedents under the Unfair Contract Terms Act.

Even if it can be shown that a disclaimer of liability is unenforceable, or if the contract does not contain a disclaimer, there is still the need to show that loss or damage arose as a result of negligence on the part of the software supplier. Here, the burden of proof normally lies with the claimant — the software user who has suffered the loss or damage — and proof is not easy, especially in an industry where there are no generally acceptable professional qualifications or standards.

Going one further step, the amount of loss or damage that may be recoverable from the Licensor, even if negligence is proved, will be affected by a number of factors, such as remoteness, contributory negligence by the claimant, and whether circumstances giving rise to the loss or damage could reasonably have been foreseen.

3.3.6 Warranties

There is obviously little incentive to a software supplier to invite claims by including warranties of any kind in his standard software contract. Nevertheless, some of the most important warranties can be implied.

Right to Grant Licence

The first is that the supplier has the right to permit the use of the program: that is to say, that he owns the copyright, or has been given authority by the copyright owner. It is obviously of prime importance to a user that he gets a valid right to use a program, since otherwise he may be prevented from using it by the rightful owner.

Performance

We have previously mentioned program performance and error correction. It would be unusual for a software supplier to warrant that his program will perform exactly to specification in all circumstances, and generally it can be said that any warranty as to performance can be replaced by the provision of a satisfactory error correction service. Similarly, a contract may exclude any representations or descriptions not forming part of the contract.

3.3.7 Indemnities

Where a contract contains no explicit warranties, there may nevertheless be indemnities. Whereas breach of a warranty, particularly as to title, may render a complete contract null and void, replacement of a warranty by an indemnity will generally mean that the contract remains in force, but the user who suffers will be entitled to compensation or mitigation. In the context of software contracts, an indemnity is probably to be preferred to an explicit warranty, but any conditions attached to the indemnity need to be carefully examined.

3.3.8 Proper Law

The whole of this section of the booklet, dealing with legal aspects of software contracts, is based on English law, and it would be impossible to deal adequately with software contracts under foreign laws. However, some users may be using software originating overseas, and many software suppliers will want to license the use of their packages to overseas customers. Despite the various international copyright conventions, it cannot be assumed that computer programs are protected in the same way under the copyright laws of all countries.

There are many differences also in the law of contract in different countries. In any software contract (or any contract of any kind) between parties in more than one country, the law which is to be applied to the contract, and by which the contract is to be construed should be stated. Obviously, a user will prefer the proper law to be that of his country. But this may not always be acceptable, and if any foreign law is to apply, then all that can be said is — beware!

3.3.9 Arbitration

Some contracts will provide that all disputes are to be settled by arbitration, and a lot of people may be happy with such a provision, as they think that arbitration is a cheap, easy and fair way of settling disputes. This is not necessarily the case, and it is interesting to see how often a dispute which goes to arbitration eventually ends up in the courts. Naturally, the sums of money at stake in disputes under software contracts are rarely big enough to warrant expensive litigation. There is a danger, however, in the belief that a software contract necessarily requires a computer professional as an arbitrator. Arbitration decisions go to the courts on points of law, and if the intention of an arbitration clause is to avoid the courts, then the arbitrator, or at least one of the arbitrators, should have a knowledge of the law. If settlement of a dispute requires a knowledge of computing, then an expert can be called in to give advice.

Generally, it is better not to have an arbitration clause in a software contract. Any form of legal action is usually costly and time-consuming. If a dispute arises which cannot be settled by negotiation, it may be possible to arrange for an independent person to mediate. If attempts to reach an agreed settlement fail, the parties may still agree to arbitration, but if this, too, cannot be agreed, then the aggrieved party may take action through the courts.

3.4 SOFTWARE DEVELOPMENT CONTRACTS (BESPOKE SOFTWARE)

3.4.1 Copyright

It has been pointed out earlier that, in the absence of other agreement, copyright in a program and documentation written by a software supplier under a development contract belongs to the supplier. If the development contract is silent on the subject of ownership of copyright, then our earlier comments on rights of use apply. In addition, the buyer of the supplier's development services may want to ensure that his program cannot be used by competitors, and further, that he has the right to permit its use by his associates or successors in business. These matters must be taken care of in the contract, bearing in mind that any act which is restricted under copyright, and which is not specifically permitted by licence or contract, is an infringement of copyright.

When a development contract provides that copyright in the finished software shall belong to the buyer, the software developer may still want certain rights. For example, he will not want to be restricted from using parts of the program in software developed for other clients; and he may ask for a prior right to market the program to others if it can be generalised and would not damage the original user's business. Where it is part of a development contract that copyright shall belong to the buyer, and the developer has certain rights of use and copying, then the roles of Licensor and Licensee are reversed. The buyer of the software becomes the Licensor, granting rights to the software developer who is then the Licensee.

3.4.2 Failure to Complete

There are two areas of particular difficulty in a development contract. The first involves rights in a partially-developed software in the event of the contractor's financial failure and inability to complete. Generally it can be said that the commissioner of the software will not have a clear and automatic right to the exclusive use of, or the copyright in, that part of the software which was completed at the time of the failure, even though progress payments have been made. The partially developed material is an asset of the failed company which will be under the control of the receiver. If there is a risk of a contractor getting into financial difficulties, there is much to be said for completed parts of the software to be handed over periodically during development.

At the same time, bespoke software developed to meet the specific requirements of a particular client is unlikely to be of commercial value to others, and the client should have little difficulty in obtaining rights of use, or copyright, from the receiver. The main problem is in the delay to the development of the software, and this can only be mitigated by having access to those parts of the work which had been completed.

3.4.3 Joint Developments

A second area of difficulty arises in joint developments. A user may either hire additional analysts and programmers from an outside organisation, or may obtain the services of a software house, to augment his own staff and to work alongside them. Who, then, owns the copyright in the finished product?

Unless the parts developed by each of the two parties involved can be separately identified (in which case each party owns the copyright in his own work), there is joint ownership of copyright. Either individual part ownership or joint ownership can create problems when it comes to rights of use or protection of the software against unauthorised use; in all cases of this type it is preferable that copyright in the software is clearly vested, by contract, in one of the parties involved, with, if necessary, a licensing of rights to the other.

3.4.4 System and Program Specification

Perhaps the most important part of a software development contract consists of the system and program specification. Two points can be made:

— the specification must be 'frozen' at the time of entering into the contract, so that both parties are clearly aware at that time of what is to be done, the cost of doing it, and the time allowed for completion;

— the contract should contain provision for amending the specification during development, coupled with a procedure for changing the price to be paid, and the time for completion, if necessary.

3.4.5 Delay

Many software development contracts run into trouble because of failure by the contractor to complete on time. People talk of penalty clauses in this connection but in fact any financial sanction on the contractor must be a genuine estimate of the loss or damage (known as liquidated damages) which the future user of the program is likely to suffer as a result of delay. However, in many cases delays occur because the user changes his mind during the development, or because information comes to light which was not made known to the contractor when the contract was entered into.

If a development is to proceed smoothly and with minimum delay and dispute, there should be set down in the

contract the names of individuals from each party who will
be responsible for liaison and progress monitoring. Even
more important, perhaps, these individuals should be able
to work together for the common purpose. The potential
user of the software should have a contractual right to
object to any of the contractor's staff employed on the
development, and to have them replaced. But it must be
recognised that this, of itself, could bring about a delay, and
it is better to have the opportunity to interview the
contractor's staff before work starts, and to ensure as far as
possible that they will be acceptable to your own staff.

3.4.6 Staff Changes

Either party, of course, must have the right to change
people employed on the development of this is made
necessary because of promotion, sickness, or termination of
employment. The software user should have a right to accept or reject any replacement proposed by the contractor.

3.4.7 Termination

There may come a stage at which, despite all precautions,
the development work is falling further and further behind,
and the quality of work being done by the contractor is
unacceptable. The commissioner of the software must have
a contractual right to terminate the contract if things go
badly wrong. Coupled with a right of termination should be
a detailed statement of the rights and obligations of each
party if the termination clause is invoked. The user, for
example, will want to acquire rights in that part of the
software which has been finished, so that he can continue
with the development and use the completed product. And
the contractor will want paying at a fair rate for the work he
has done and handed over.

References

The Copyright Act, 1956

Report of the Committee to Consider the Law on Copyright and Designs (The Whitford Committee), Cmnd 6732, March 1977

Computer Installation Contracts, Computerguide 12, NCC Publications, 1977

Model Form of Conditions of Contract for the Supply and Installation (Purchase) of Computer Equipment, Institute of Purchasing and Supply, 1979

Shortened Form of Model Form of Conditions of Contract for the Supply and Installation (Purchase) of Computer Equipment, Institute of Purchasing and Supply, 1979

E. R. Sambridge, *Purchasing Computers,* Gower Press, 1979

J. D. Lomax, *Documentation of Software Products,* NCC Publications, 1977